Collectible

FLORIDA SHELLS

R. Tucker Abbott, Ph.D.

CONTENTS

© 1984 BY AMERICAN MALACOLOGISTS, INC.
ALL RIGHTS RESERVED. P.O. BOX 2255 MELBOURNE, FL 32902
ISBN-0-915826-11-9   NINTH PRINTING, 1995

Conchs

The PINK CONCH is an abundant source of protein in the Bahamas and Lower Florida Keys where the foot is used in chowders and salads. The shell reaches a length of about 8 inches (20 cm). This cut-away shows the internal whorls. *Strombus gigas* (Linnaeus, 1758).

NOTE: In order to build up populations again, there is a ban at present on collecting live Pink Conchs in Florida.

A 1990 Florida law requires a fishing license (obtainable from tackle shops) for those 16 to 65 years of age who collect live shells from a boat or at a depth below 4 feet.

On Sanibel Island, southwest Florida, there is a ban on collecting any live shells, except for certain edible bivalves.

The 3-inch-long FIGHTING CONCH *(Strombus alatus* Gmelin, 1791) is common in shallow water in southern and west Florida. They feed on algae. Eyes are at the end of the tentacles.

Alice Barlow, photo

Conchs

Conchs live in colonies in sand and weedy areas. The sickle-shaped operculum at the end of the foot assists the conch in crawling and to ward off enemies.

Dwarf
HAWK-WING
CONCH

WEST INDIAN FIGHTING CONCH
Strombus pugilis Linnaeus, 1758.
Uncommon in S. E. Florida
Common in West Indies. 3'' (7cm).

HAWK-WING CONCH
Strombus raninus Gmelin, 1791.
South Florida - West Indies.
Common. 3.5'' (9 cm).

MILK CONCH. 4 - 6'' (14 cm)
Strombus costatus Gmelin, 1791
Uncommon in S. Florida

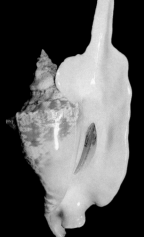

FLORIDA FIGHTING CONCH. 3''
Strombus alatus Gmelin, 1791
Carolinas to Texas. Common in
shallow water

ROOSTER-TAIL CONCH. 5'' (12 cm).
Strombus gallus Linnaeus, 1758.
Rare in Florida; locally
common in Caribbean

Helmets

These large, slow-moving snails live in sandy areas and feed on sea urchins and sea biscuits (echinoderms). Cameos are made from large helmets.

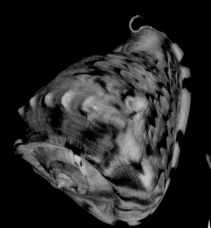

KING HELMET. 4 - 8'' (20 cm).
Cassis tuberosa (Linnaeus, 1758)
Carolinas to Brazil. Rare
in Florida.

QUEEN HELMET. 8 - 11'' (25 cm).
Cassis madagascariensis
Lamarck, 1822. Carolinas - West
Indies. Becoming rare in Florida.

FLAME HELMET. 4'' (10 cm).
Cassis flammea
(Linnaeus, 1758). Rare
in S. Florida. Common
in West Indies.

The SCOTCH BONNET is the
state shell of North Carolina
Bonnets have a fan-shaped trapdoor.

Bonnets

Tuns

Tuns have light-weight,
spirally ridged shells. No
trapdoor present. Tuns feed
on sea-cucumbers.

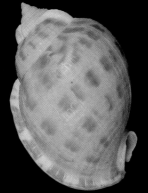

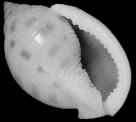

SCOTCH BONNET, sometimes
is smooth (above). *Phalium
granulatum* (Born, 1778) 3'' (8 cm).
North Carolina to West Indies.

ROYAL BONNET. 2'' (5 cm).
Sconsia striata (Lamarck,
1816). Trawlers bring this
in from deepwater.

ATLANTIC MORUM. 1'' (2.5 cm).
Morum oniscus (Linnaeus,
1767). S. E. Florida - West
Indies. Uncommon, under rocks.

GIANT TUN. 5 - 7'' (17 cm).
Tonna galea (Linnaeus, 1758).
Carolinas to Texas. Common

ATLANTIC PARTRIDGE TUN. 3''
Tonna maculosa (Dillwyn,
1817). S.E. Florida to Brazil.
Uncommon in shallow water

Tritons

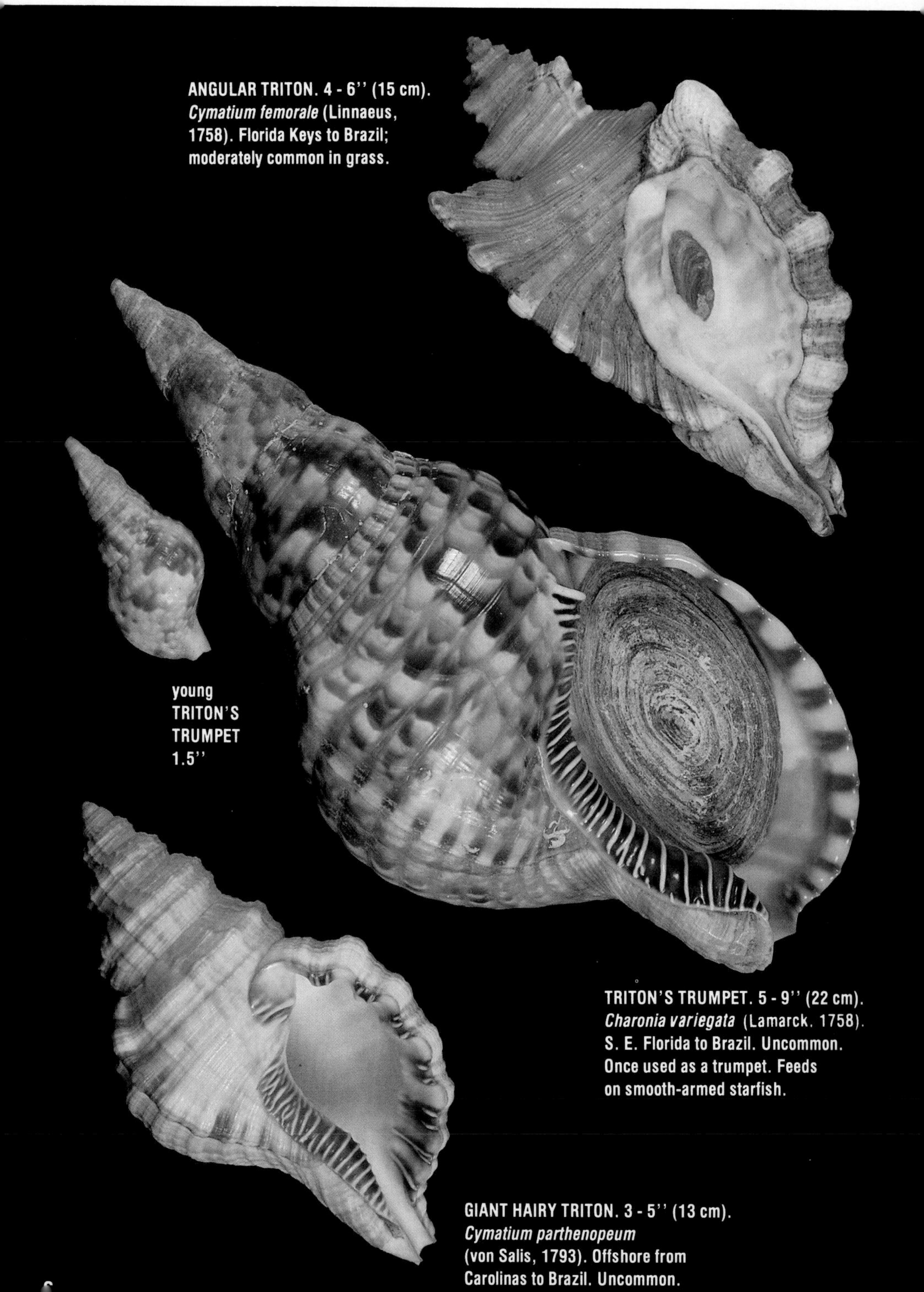

ANGULAR TRITON. 4 - 6'' (15 cm).
Cymatium femorale (Linnaeus,
1758). Florida Keys to Brazil;
moderately common in grass.

young
TRITON'S
TRUMPET
1.5''

TRITON'S TRUMPET. 5 - 9'' (22 cm).
Charonia variegata (Lamarck. 1758).
S. E. Florida to Brazil. Uncommon.
Once used as a trumpet. Feeds
on smooth-armed starfish.

GIANT HAIRY TRITON. 3 - 5'' (13 cm).
Cymatium parthenopeum
(von Salis, 1793). Offshore from
Carolinas to Brazil. Uncommon.

Hairy Tritons

DOG-HEAD TRITON. 2'' (5 cm). *Cymatium caribbaeum* Clench & Turner, 1957. Carolinas to Brazil. Shallow water; uncommon.

Two variations of the ATLANTIC HAIRY TRITON. 2 - 3'' (8 cm). Carolinas to Texas to Brazil. Moderately common under rocks. *Cymatium pileare* (Linnaeus, 1758).

KREBS' HAIRY TRITON. 1'' *C. krebsii* (Mörch, 1877). S.E. Florida - Caribbean. Subtidal on sand. Uncommon.

POULSON'S TRITON. 2'' (5 cm). *Cymatium cingulatum* (Lamarck, 1822). Carolinas to Texas to Brazil. Uncommon.

GOLD-MOUTHED TRITON. 1½'' *C. nicobaricum* (Roding, 1798). S. E. Florida to Brazil. Common; under rocks, intertidal.

KNOBBED TRITON 1 - 2'' (4 cm). *C. muricinum* (Röding, 1798). S. E. Florida to Brazil. Subtidal, on sand. Common.

Frog-Shells

The frog shells of the family Bursidae have a small funnel at the top of the opening.

Distorsios

The related distorsio frog shells have a twisted body and gnarled opening.

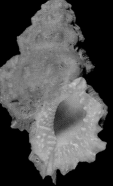

GRANULAR FROG-SHELL 2'' (5 cm). *Bursa granularis* (Röding, 1798). S.E. Florida to Brazil. Common.

GAUDY FROG-SHELL *Bursa corrugata* (Perry, 1811). 2'' (5 cm). S. E. Florida to Brazil. Uncommon; subtidal.

ST. THOMAS FROG-SHELL 1'' (2.5 cm). *Bursa thomae* (Orbigny, 1842). Carolinas to Brazil; rare.

CHESTNUT FROG-SHELL 2'' (5 cm). *Bursa bufo* (Bruguière, 1792). Offshore; uncommon.

ATLANTIC DISTORSIO. 3'' (7 cm). *Distorsio clathrata* (Lamarck, 1816). Carolinas to Texas to Brazil. Offshore; uncommon

MC GINTY'S DISTORSIO. 1.5'' (4 cm). *Distorsio macgintyi* Emerson and Puffer, 1953. Carolinas to Brazil. Offshore; uncommon

The JUNONIA is the pride of Sanibel Island,
but is also found offshore from the Carolinas to Texas.
Scaphellas are usually in deepwater. Spotted animal
has no trapdoor (operculum).

Volutes

JUNONIA. 2 - 3.5'' (9 cm).
Scaphella junonia (Lamarck, 1804).
Carolinas to Texas. Offshore; uncommon.

BUTLER'S VOLUTE. 4 - 5'' (12 cm).
is subspecies of the JUNONIA
(*butleri* Clench, 1953) from west
Gulf of Mexico. Uncommon.

GOULD'S VOLUTE. 2 - 3''' (6 cm).
Scaphella gouldiana Dall,
1887. Off south Florida. Rare
Comes spotted also.

KIENER'S VOLUTE. 8'' (20 cm).
Scaphella dubia subspecies

DUBIOUS VOLUTE. 3'' (8 cm).
Scaphella dubia (Broderip,
1827. S. E. United States

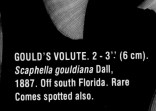

Tulips

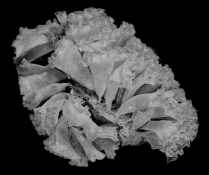

Mass of horny capsules containing hundreds of eggs of a Tulip Shell.

TRUE TULIP. 4 - 6'' (14 cm).
Fasciolaria tulipa
(Linnaeus, 1758). Carolinas
to Florida Keys; Caribbean. Common.

BANDED TULIP. 2 - 3'' (7 cm)
Fasciolaria hunteria (Perry, 1811).
Carolinas to Alabama. Common
in shallow, grassy bays.

TORTUGAS BANDED TULIP. 3'' (7 cm).
Fasciolaria lilium subspecies
tortugana Hollister, 1957.
Off Tortugas Island, Florida. Uncommon

BRANHAM'S BANDED TULIP. 4'' (10 cm).
F. lilium subspecies *branhamae*
Rehder and Abbott, 1951. Gulf of Mexico.
Uncommon; deepwater

Crown Conchs

A single species is found from all of Florida to Texas, usually among mangroves and oysters in sheltered bays. From one colony to another, they vary in size, color and shape. Smallest comes from Lower Florida Keys. *Melongena corona* (Gmelin, 1791). 3''.

Mangrove habitat of Crown Conchs

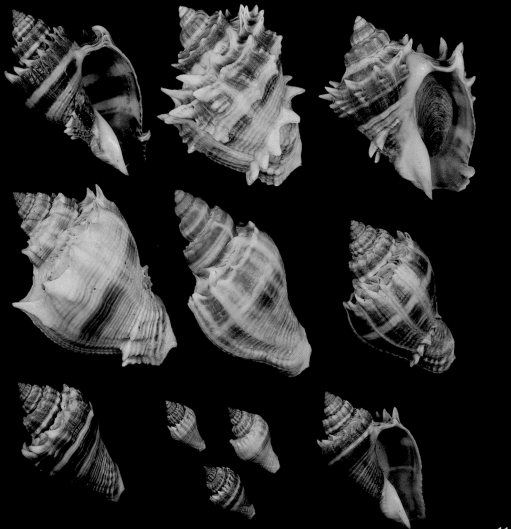

young

GIANT EASTERN MUREX
Hexaplex fulvescens
(Sowerby, 1834). Carolinas
to Texas. Subtidal; common
5 - 7'' (17 cm).

Murex

BEAU'S MUREX. 4'' (10 cm). *Siratus
beauii* (Fischer & Bernardi, 1857)
Florida to Brazil. Deepwater; uncommon.

LACE MUREX. 2'' (5 cm). *Chicoreus
dilectus* A. Adams, 1855. S.C. to
Florida. Common in shallow areas.

APPLE MUREX. 3'' (7.5 cm). *Phyllonotus
pomum* (Gmelin, 1791). Carolinas to
Brazil. Subtidal; common.

CABRIT'S MUREX. 2'' (5 cm).
Murex cabritii Bernardi, 1859.
Offshore, S. E. U. S. Uncommon.

ROSE MUREX. 1.5'' (4 cm).
Murex rubidus F. C. Baker,
1897. S. E. U. S. Uncommon.

HIDALGO'S MUREX. 1.5'' (4 cm).
Murexiella hidalgoi (Crosse,
1869). Offshore, S. E. Uncommon.

TRIANGULAR TYPHIS. 1''
Tripterotyphis triangularis
(A. Adams, 1855). Key West;
Caribbean. Subtidal rocks; rare.

LITTLE ASPELLA. 1'' (2.5 cm).
Aspella paupercula (C. B. Adams,
1850). Carolinas to Barbados.
Subtidal rocks; uncommon.

PITTED MUREX. 1'' (2.5 cm).
Favartia cellulosa (Conrad,
1846). Carolinas to Brazil.
Subtidal rocks; common.

PAZ'S MUREX. 1.5'' (4 cm).
Poirieria pazi (Crosse, 1869).
East Florida and Caribbean.
Offshore; uncommon to rare.

HEXAGONAL MUREX. 1'' (2.5 cm).
Muricopsis oxytatus (Smith,
1938). Florida and West Indies.

MANSFIELD'S LATIAXIS
Latiaxis mansfieldi
(McGinty, 1940). 1''
S. E. U. S., offshore. Rare.

SHORT CORAL-SHELL. 1'' (2.5 cm).
Coralliophila abbreviata
(Lamarck, 1816). S. E. Florida
to Brazil. Coral reefs; Common.

DALL'S LATIAXIS. 1.5''
Latiaxis dalli (Emerson
& D'Attilio, 1963). Gulf of
Mexico. Deepwater. Rare.

Rock-Shells & Drills

The rock-dwelling Purpura snails and most Murex produce a liquid dye.
Drills and rock-shells bore holes in bivalves and suck out the soft insides.

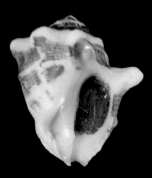

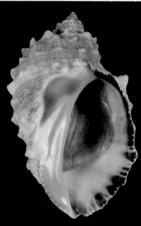

DELTOID ROCK-SHELL. 1'' (2.5 cm).
Thais deltoidea (Lamarck, 1822).
S. E. Florida to Brazil. Intertidal
rocks. Common.

WIDE-MOUTHED PURPURA. 2'' (5 cm).
Purpura patula (Linnaeus,
1758). S. E. Florida and West
Indies. Intertidal rocks; common.

RUSTIC ROCK-SHELL. 1'' (2.5 cm).
Thais rustica (Lamarck, 1822).
S. E. Florida to Brazil.
Intertidal rocks; common.

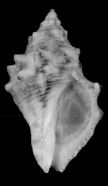

FLORIDA ROCK-SHELL. 2'' (5 cm). Knobbed and smooth
variety. *Thais haemastoma* subspecies *floridana*
(Conrad, 1837). Estuarine rocks, and oyster beds. Common.

ATLANTIC OYSTER DRILL. 1'' (2.5 cm). *Urosalpinx cinereus*
(Say, 1822). Eastern Canada to N. E. Florida. Oyster beds.
Common.

GULF OYSTER DRILL. 1''
Urosalpinx perrugata
(Conrad, 1846). Both sides
of Florida. Intertidal. Common.

MAUVE-MOUTH DRILL. 1''
Calotrophon ostrearum (Conrad,
1846). Florida. Intertidal rocks.

THICK-LIPPED DRILL. 1''
Eupleura caudata (Say,

SHARP-RIBBED DRILL. .4''
Eupleura sulcidentata
Dall, 1890. Florida. Off
shore. Uncommon.

Whelks

In Florida, members of the genus BUSYCON are called whelks. Females lay chains of leathery capsules each containing eggs or baby shells.

KIENER'S WHELK. 5 - 8'' (20 cm). *Busycon carica* subspecies *eliceans* (Montfort, 1810). N. E. Florida. Offshore, common.

immature

LIGHTNING WHELK and its string of egg capsules. 5 - 16'' (40 cm). *Busycon contrarium* (Conrad, 1840). Usually left-handed (sinistral). New Jersey to Texas. Subtidal. Common.

TURNIP WHELK. 4'' (10 cm). *Busycon coarctatum* (Sowerby, 1825). S.W. Gulf of Mexico. Rare.

PEAR WHELK. 3 - 4'' (9 cm).

CHANNELED WHELK. 6'' (15 cm). *Busycon*

Cones

Cones are one of the most popular families among shell collectors. There are about 40 Caribbean species and about 350 worldwide. They feed on live fish, worms and other mollusks, using a poison and harpoonlike tooth. Only Indo-Pacific species have caused human deaths, but Atlantic ones can sting.

GLORY-OF-THE-ATLANTIC. 1.5'' (4 cm). *Conus granulatus* Linnaeus, 1758. Rare.

JASPER CONE. ½'' (1.3 cm). *Conus jaspideus* Gmelin, 1791. Florida to Brazil. Shallow water; common in sand.

STEARN'S CONE. ½'' (1.3 cm). *Conus jaspideus subspecies. stearnsi* Conrad, 1869. Carolinas to Gulf of Mexico. Shallows; common.

MOUSE CONE. 1'' (2.5 cm). *Conus mus* Hwass, 1792. S. E. Florida and West Indies Shore reef flats; common.

VILLEPIN'S CONE 2'' (5 cm). *Conus villepini* Fischer & Bernardi, 1857.

Variations of the FLORIDA CONE. 1½'' (4 cm). *Conus floridanus* Gabb, 1868. Carolinas to both sides of Florida. Intertidal to offshore. Common.

CROWN CONE. 2'' (5 cm). *Conus regius* Gmelin, 1791. S.E. U.S. to Brazil. Shallow reef waters under rocks; common. Rarely yellow.

ALPHABET CONE. 2'' (5 cm). *Conus spurius* Gmelin, 1791. S.E. U.S. and West Indies. Subtidal in sand; common. Orange-banded form rare.

Variations in color in **SOZON'S CONE** 2½'' (6 cm). *Conus delessertii* Recluz, 1843. Off Carolinas to the Gulf of Mexico. Locally common.

AUSTIN'S CONE. 2'' (5 cm). *Conus cancellatus* Hwass, 1792. Gulf of Mexico; deepwater. Uncommon.

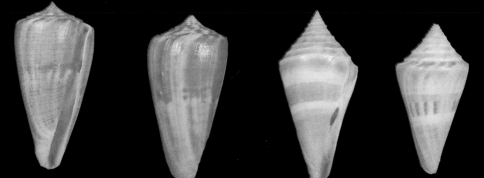

JULIA CLENCH'S CONE. 1½'' (4 cm). *Conus amphiurgus* Dall, form *juliae* Clench, 1942. Offshore, S.E. U.S. and West Indies. Uncommon.

STIMPSON'S CONE. 2'' (5 cm). *Conus stimpsoni* Dall, 1902. S.E. U.S. and Gulf of Mexico. Deepwater; uncommon.

Moon Snails

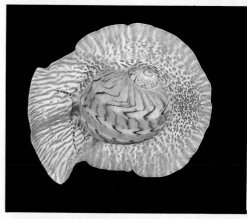

Living animal, GAUDY NATICA, *Natica canrena L.*

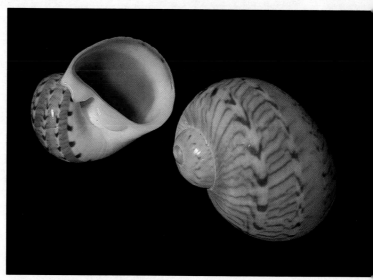

GAUDY NATICA 1½'' (4 cm).
Natica canrena
(Linnaeus, 1758).
Carolinas to West Indies.
Sandy shallows; common.
Trapdoor shelly.

Alice Barlow, photos

SHARK'S EYE 2½'' (6 cm)
Polinices duplicatus
(Say, 1822). Eastern U.S.
Sandy shallows;
common. Sandy ''collar''
is its egg mass.

18

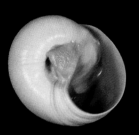

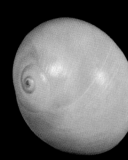

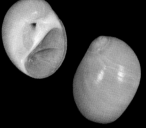

SHARK'S EYE (or Atlantic Moon). 2½'' (6 cm).
Polinices duplicatus (Say, 1822). Eastern
U.S. Sandy shallows. Common.

BROWN MOON-SNAIL. 1½'' (6 cm).
Polinices hepaticus (Röding,
1798). S.E. U.S. (rare); West
Indies. Sandy shallows. Uncommon.

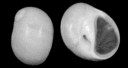

MILK MOON-SNAIL. 1'' (2.5 cm).
Polinices lacteus (Guilding,
1834). Carolinas to Brazil.
Sandy shallows; common.

GAUDY NATICA. 1'' (2.5 cm).
Natica canrena (Linnaeus, 1758).
Carolinas to West Indies. Sandy
shallows; common.

LIVID NATICA. ½'' (1.2 cm).
Natica livida Pfeiffer,
1840. S. Florida to
Brazil. Shallows; common.

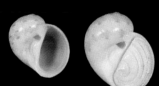

FLORIDA NATICA 1'' (2.5 cm).
Natica floridana (Rehder, 1943).
S. E. Florida to Brazil.
Offshore in sand. Uncommon.

SULCATE NATICA ¾'' (2 cm).
Stigmaulax sulcatus (Born,
1778). Florida; West Indies. Rare.

PHILIPPI'S NUTMEG. 1'' (2.5 cm).
Trigonostoma tenerum
(Philippi, 1848). Florida. Uncommon.

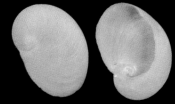

BABY'S EAR MOON. 1½'' (4 cm).
Sinum perspectivum (Say, 1831).

MACULATED EAR MOON. 1½''
(4 cm). *Sinum maculosum*

COMMON NUTMEG. 1½'' (4 cm).
Cancellaria reticulata (Linnaeus

Marginellas

The small, glossy marginellas
travel rapidly over sandy bottoms
in search of dead meat. There
are dozens of species in Florida.

George Raeihle, photo

WHITE-SPOTTED MARGINELLA. ½'' (1.3 cm). *Marginella guttata* Dillwyn, 1817. S. E. Florida; West Indies. Common.

ORANGE MARGINELLA. ¾'' (2 cm). *Marginella carnea* (Storer, 1837). S. E. Florida; West Indies. Sandy shallows; uncommon.

BOREAL MARGINELLA. ½'' (1.3 cm). *Marginella roscida* Redfield, 1860. Eastern United States. Sandy shallows off beaches. Uncommon.

COMMON ATLANTIC MARGINELLA *Marginella apicina* Menke, 1828. ⅓'' (1 cm). Carolinas to Texas. Sandy shallows. Common.

CARMINE MARGINELLA *M. hematita* Kiener, 1834. Carolinas to Brazil. Rare.

ORANGE-BANDED MARGINELLA *Hyalina avena* (Kiener, 1834). Carolinas to Brazil. Common.

Living ATLANTIC MARGINELLA

Olives

The glossy olive shells are found in sandy shallows. They feed on dead shrimp and fish. There are two species in Florida. They do not have an operculum.

LETTERED OLIVE with erect siphon.

Color variations in the LETTERED OLIVE, *Oliva sayana* Ravenel, 1834, from S. E. United States. 2 - 3'' (6 cm). Common in sandy areas, especially on the west coast of Florida.

Color variations in the NETTED OLIVE, *Oliva reticularis* Lamarck, 1810. Off coral sand beaches, S. E. Florida; West Indies. 2'' (5 cm).

WEST INDIAN DWARF OLIVE *Olivella nivea* (Gmelin, 1791). 1'' (2 - 5 cm). S. E. Florida; West Indies. Sandy shallows; common. No operculum.

Florida Horse Conch

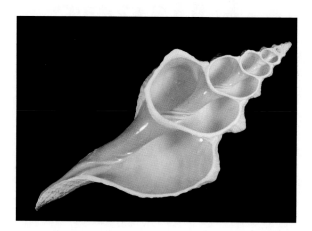

FLORIDA HORSE CONCH is the official
representative shell of the State of Florida.
It lives throughout the waters of Florida
from depths of one to 80 feet. They feed on
clams. *Pleuroploca gigantea* (Kiener,
1840). Up to 24 inches. Carolinas to Texas.

Nerites

Nerites live on rocky shores, and are vegetarians feeding on minute algae. Their trapdoors are shelly.

Virgin Nerites swarming on intertidal flats.

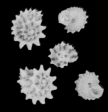

SMOOTH ATLANTIC TEGULA. ½'' (1.3 cm). *Tegula fasciata* (Born, 1778). South Florida to Brazil. Subtidal rocks; common. In family Trochidae.

BLEEDING TOOTH. 1'' (2.5 cm). *Nerita peloronta* Linnaeus, 1758. Florida Keys; West Indies. Intertidal rocky shores.

STAR ARENE. ¼'' (0.5 cm). *Arene cruentata* (Mühlfeld, 1829). S. E. Florida; West Indies. Subtidal rocks; uncommon.

OLIVE NERITE. ½'' (1.3 cm). *Neritina reclivata* (Say, 1822) Florida to Texas. Brackish water on mud. Common.

FOUR-TOOTHED NERITE. ¾'' (2 cm). *Nerita versicolor* Gmelin, 1791. South Florida; West Indies. Common on shore rocks.

VIRGIN NERITE. ½'' (1.3 cm). *Neritina virginea* (Linnaeus, 1758). Florida to Texas to Brazil. Intertidal mud flats. Common.

ANTILLEAN NERITE. ¾'' (2 cm). *Nerita fulgurans* Gmelin, 1791. S. E. Florida to Texas to Brazil. Brackish sands. Locally common.

TESSELLATE NERITE ¾'' (2 cm). *Nerita tessellata* Gmelin, 1791. Florida to Brazil. Intertidal rock pools. Common.

EMERALD NERITE. ¼'' (0.5 cm). *Smaragdia viridis* (Linnaeus, 1758). S. E. Florida; West Indies. Eelgrass beds. Common.

23

Flamingo Tongue

Reef scene in the Florida Keys. At left is stinging coral. Do not touch! To the right is the FLAMINGO TONGUE that lives on seafans. Never collect more than two, if at all. This species is being over-collected.

Live FLAMING TONGUE. 1'' (2.5 cm). Spotted mantle makes shell.

Bubble Shells

ATLANTIC BUBBLE. 1'' (2 - 5 cm). *Bulla striata* Bruguiere, 1792. Florida to Texas to Brazil. Quiet, grassy areas. Common.

BROWN-LINED PAPER-BUBBLE. 1½'' (4 cm). *Hydatina vesicaria* (Lightfoot, 1786). South Florida to Brazil. Uncommon. See back cover for living specimen.

FLAMINGO TONGUE. 1'' (2.5 cm). *Cyphoma gibbosum* (Linnaeus, 1758). Florida Keys; West Indies. On seafans. Common.

Carrier Shells

Carrier-shells pick up other small shells and bits of coral, and, with their mantles, cement them to their own shells. This serves as a camouflage, The operculum, or trapdoor, is horny.

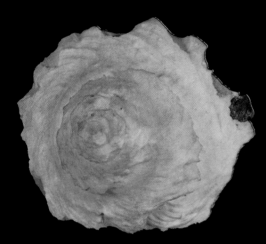

LONGLEY'S CARRIER-SHELL. 5'' (25 cm).
Xenophora longleyi Bartsch, 1931.
Off the Carolinas to the West Indies.
Deepwater; rare. Whorls overhang.

CARIBBEAN CARRIER-SHELL. 2.5'' (6 cm).
Xenophora caribaea Petit, 1857.
Gulf of Mexico to Brazil. Deepwater; uncommon.
Small, neat umbilicus on underside.

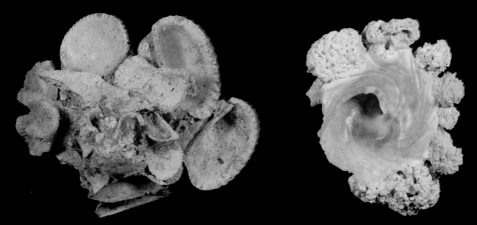

ATLANTIC CARRIER-SHELL. 2'' (5 cm). *Xenophora conchyliophora* (Born, 1780).
Carolinas to Texas and to Brazil. Shallow water. Moderately common.

Spindles & Vases

ORNAMENTED SPINDLE. 3'' (7 cm).
Fusinus eucosmius (Dall, 1889).
Deepwater; both sides of
Florida to Texas. Uncommon.

TOM DOW'S SPINDLE. 4'' (10 cm).
Fusinus dowianus Olsson, 1954.
Gulf of Mexico; West Indies.
Deepwater; uncommon.

COUE'S SPINDLE. 5'' (13 cm).
Fusinus couei (Petit, 1853).
Gulf of Mexico. Deepwater;
uncommon.

TURNIP SPINDLE. 6'' (15 cm).
Fusinus timessus (Dall,
1889). Deepwater; both sides
of Florida to Texas. Uncommon.

BROWN-LINED LATIRUS.

TROCHLEAR LATIRUS. 2''　CHESTNUT LATIRUS 1½'' (4 cm)

Wentletraps Janthinas
Worm-Shells

ANGULATE WENTLETRAP
1'' (2.5 cm). *Epitonium angulatum* (Say, 1830). Eastern U.S. Shallow sandy bays. Common.

LAMELLOSE WENTLETRAP
1'' (2.5 cm). *Epitonium lamellosum* (Lamarck, 1822). Florida; West Indies. Common.

DALL'S WENTLETRAP
1'' (2.5 cm). *Cirsotrema dalli* Rehder, 1945. S.E. U.S. Uncommon.

MITCHELL'S WENTLETRAP
2'' (5 cm). *Amaea mitchelli* (Dall, 1896). Florida to Texas. Uncommon.

NOBLE WENTLETRAP
1½'' (4 cm). *Sthenorytis pernobilis* (Fisch. & Bern., 1857) Deepwater. S.E. U.S.; West Indies. Rare.

COMMON JANTHINA. 1½'' (4 cm). *Janthina janthina* (Linnaeus, 1758). Worldwide warm seas. Floats with self-made bubbles. Common.

PALLID JANTHINA. 1'' (2.5 cm). *Janthina pallida* (Thompson, 1840). Worldwide warm seas. Often cast ashore. Common. Pelagic.

ELONGATE JANTHINA. 1'' (2.5 cm). *Janthina globosa* Swainson, 1822 Worldwide warm seas. Common. Pelagic.

FLORIDA WORM-SHELL. 4'' (10 cm). *Vermicularia knorri* (Deshayes, 1843). Carolinas to Gulf of Mexico. Common.

SLIT WORM-SHELL. 3'' (8 cm). *Siliquaria squamata* (Blainville, 1827). Offshore in sponges. Carolinas to Brazil. Uncommon.

IRREGULAR WORM-SHELL. 3'' (8 cm). *Dendropoma irregularis* (Orbigny, 1842).. S.E. Florida to Brazil. Forms masses on rocks.

Dove Shells
Nassa Snails
Trivias

COMMON DOVE-SHELL. ½'' (1.3 cm). Very variable in color pattern. *Columbella mercatoria* (Linnaeus, 1758). Eastern Florida to Brazil. On shallow-water weeds. Abundant.

COMMON EASTERN NASSA. ½'' (1.3 cm). *Nassarius vibex* (Say, 1822). Eastern United States. Muddy sand flats. Common.

WELL-RIBBED DOVE-SHELL. ½'' (1.3 cm). *Anachis lafresnayi* (Fischer & Bernardi, 1856). Maine to Texas; common.

SHARP-KNOBBED NASSA. ¼'' (0.5 cm). *Nassarius acutus* (Say, 1822). Florida to Texas. Shallow bays. Common.

VARIABLE NASSA. ½'' (1.3 cm). *Nassarius albus* (Say, 1826). Carolinas to Brazil. Shallow sands. Common.

COFFEE BEAN TRIVIA. ½'' (1.3 cm). *Trivia pediculus* (Linnaeus, 1758).

WHITE GLOBE TRIVIA. ⅓'' (1 cm). *Trivia nix* (Schilder, 1922). Florida to Brazil. Reefs; rare

Ceriths
Periwinkles
Niso - Turritella

FLORIDA CERITH. 1'' (2.5 cm).
Cerithium atratum (Born, 1778).
Carolinas to Texas to Brazil.
Shallow water; common.

STOCKY CERITH. 1'' (2.5 cm).
Cerithium litteratum (Born,
1778). S.E. Florida to Brazil.
Shallow reef areas; common.

FALSE CERITH. ½''(1.3 cm).
Batillaria minima (Gmelin, 1791).
South Florida to Brazil.
Abundant on mud.

FLY-SPECKED CERITH.
1'' (2.5 cm). Cerithium
muscarum Say, 1832.
S. Florida to Brazil.

BEADED PERIWINKLE. ¾''
Tectarius muricatus (Linnaeus, 1758). South Florida;
West Indies. Tidal shores.

ANGULATE PERIWINKLE. 1''
Littorina angulifera (Lamarck, 1822). Florida to Brazil. On
mangrove trees; common.

MARSH PERIWINKLE. 1''
Littorina irrorata (Say, 1822).
Eastern U.S. to Texas.
Common in marshes.

ZEBRA PERIWINKLE. ½''
Littorina ziczac (Gmelin,
1791). Florida and West
Indies. Common; shore rocks.

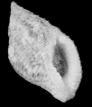

TINTED CANTHARUS. 1''
Pisania tincta (Conrad,
1846). Carolinas to Texas to

HENDERSON'S NISO. 1''
(2.5 cm). *Niso hendersoni*
Bartsch, 1953. S.E.
U.S. Offshore; uncommon.

GIANT ATLANTIC PYRAM.
¾'' (2 cm). *Pyramidella
dolabrata* (Linnaeus.

EASTERN TURRITELLA. 2''
(5 cm). *Turritella exoleta*
(Linnaeus, 1758). Carolinas
to Brazil. Offshore; common.

Slipper-Shells

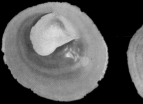 

STRIATE CUP-AND-SAUCER. 1'' (2.5 cm).
Crucibulum striatum Say, 1824.
Eastern United States. Subtidal; on rocks.
⅓ of cup attached by its side. Common.

WEST INDIAN CUP-AND-SAUCER. 1''
(2.5 cm). Crucibulum auricula (Gmelin,
1791). Carolinas to Texas to Brazil.
Offshore; attached to other shells. Uncommon.

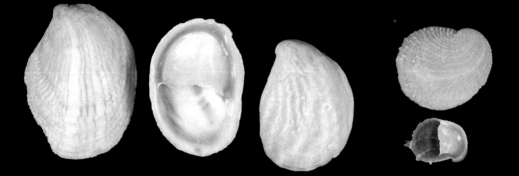

ATLANTIC SLIPPER-SHELL. 1'' (2.5 cm). *Crepidula
fornicata* (Linnaeus, 1758). Eastern U.S.
Ribbed when grows on scallops. Subtidal; common.

SPINY SLIPPERSHELL. 1'' (2.5 cm).
Crepidula aculeata (Gmelin,
1791). Carolinas to Texas
to Brazil. Shallow water;
common.

 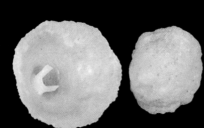 

EASTERN WHITE SLIPPER-SHELL.
½'' (1.3 cm). *Crepidula plana*
Say, 1822. Canada to Brazil.
On inside of dead shells; common.

FALSE CUP-AND-SAUCER. 1'' (2.5 cm).
Cheilea equestris (Linnaeus,
1758). Florida to Brazil

WHITE HOOF-SHELL
½'' (1.3 cm). *Hipponix
antiquatus* (Linnaeus,
1758). Florida to Brazil

Turbans & Star-Shells

CARVED STAR-SHELL.
2'' (5 cm). *Astraea caelata* (Gmelin, 1791). S.E. Florida; West Indies. Reefs; common.

GREEN STAR-SHELL. 2'' (5 cm). *Astraea tuber* (Linnaeus, 1767). S.E. Florida; West Indies. Reefs; common.

AMERICAN STAR-SHELL.
1½'' (4 cm). *Astraea americana* (Gmelin, 1791). S.E. Florida. Weedy shallows; common.

LONG-SPINED STAR-SHELL. 2'' (5 cm). *Astraea phoebia* Röding, 1798. S.E. Florida; West Indies. In weed; common.

CHESTNUT TURBAN. 1'' (2.5 cm). *Turbo castanea* Gmelin, 1791. Carolinas to Brazil. Subtidal, rough bottoms. Common. Red

Cowries

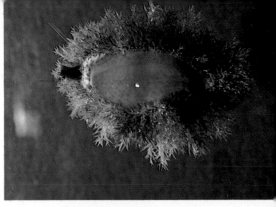

The fleshy mantle makes the glossy shell. ATLANTIC YELLOW COWRIE. ¾'' (2 cm).

ATLANTIC DEER COWRIE. 3 - 7'' (15 cm). *Cypraea cervus* Linnaeus, 1771. Carolinas to Florida; Cuba. Subtidal on rocks; common.

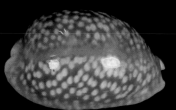

MEASLED COWRIE. 2 - 3½'' (8 cm). *Cypraea zebra* Linnaeus, 1758. S.E. Florida to Brazil. Subtidal rocks; common. Note dark ''eye'' within white spots on sides of shell.

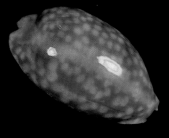

ATLANTIC GRAY COWRIE. 1'' *Cypraea cinerea* Gmelin, 1791. Carolinas to Brazil. Under ~~subtidal rocks; uncommon.~~

SURINAM COWRIE. 1'' (2.5 cm). *Cypraea surinamensis* Perry, 1811. S.E. Florida to Brazil. Deepwater; very rare.

ATLANTIC YELLOW COWRIE. ¾'' (2 cm). *Cypraea acicularis* Gmelin, 1791. Carolinas to Brazil. Subtidal, reefs; uncommon.

Top - Shells
Limpets
&
Sundials

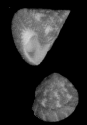

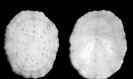

SCULPTURED TOP-SHELL.
¾'' (2 cm). *Calliostoma euglyptum* (A. Adams, 1854). Carolinas to Texas. Offshore; common.

ADELE'S TOP-SHELL. ¾'' (2 cm). *Calliostoma adelae* Schwengel, 1951. S.E. Florida. Shallows; common.

JUJUBE TOP-SHELL. 1'' (2.5 cm). *Calliostoma jujubinum* (Gmelin, 1791). Carolinas to Texas to Brazil. Common.

PSYCHE TOP-SHELL. 1½'' (4 cm). *C. psyche* Dall, 1889. Carolinas to Fla. Offshore; uncommon.

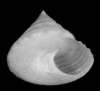

BARBADOS KEYHOLE LIMPET. 1'' (2.5 cm). *Fissurella barbadensis* (Gmelin, 1791). S.E. Florida to Brazil. Subtidal rock shores; common.

CAYENNE KEYHOLE LIMPET. 1'' (2.5 cm). *Diodora cayenensis* (Lamarck, 1822). Eastern U.S. Subtiday rocks; common.

SPOTTED ATLANTIC LIMPET. ½'' (1.3 cm). *Patelloida pustulata* (Helbling, 1779). S.E. Florida; West Indies. Subtidal rocks; common.

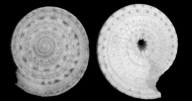

STRIPED FALSE LIMPET. 1'' (2.5 cm). *Siphonaria pectinata* (Linnaeus, 1758). Florida to Texas; Caribbean. Intertidal rocks. Common. Is a pulmonate snail.

ATLANTIC SUNDIAL. 1½'' (4 cm). *Architectonica nobilis* Röding, 1798. Carolinas to Brazil. Subtidal; moderately common.

ATLANTIC MODULUS. ½'' (2 cm). *Modulus modulus* (Linnaeus, 1758). N.C. to Texas to Brazil. Shallows; common.

33

Augers & Miters

1 - 3, *Terebra salleana* Deshayes, 1859. 4 and 5, *Terebra hastata* (Gmelin, 1791). 6, *Mitra nodulosa* (Gmelin, 1791). 7, *Vexillum pulchellum* (Reeve, 1843). 8, *Clathrodrillia solida* C.B. Adams, 1850. 9, *Mitra barbadensis* (Gmelin, 1791). 10, *Vexillum variatum* (Reeve, 1845). 11, *Terebra taurinus* (Lightfoot, 1786). 12, *Terebra floridana* Dall, 1889. 13, *Terebra dislocata* (Say, 1822). 14, *Mitra florida* Gould, 1856. ALL NATURAL SIZE.

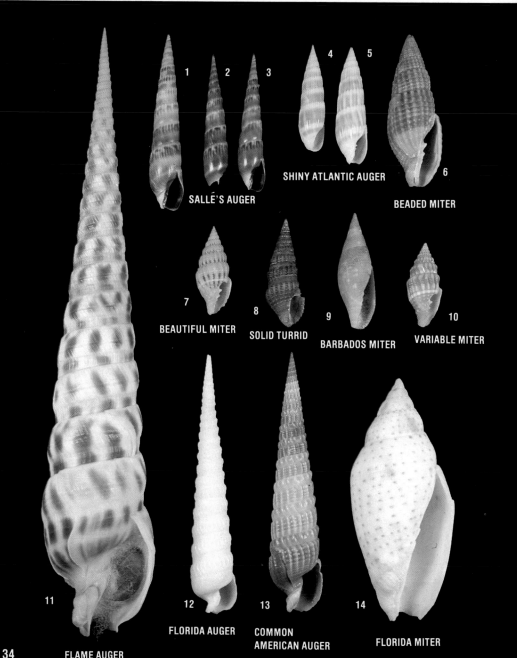

SHINY ATLANTIC AUGER

SALLÉ'S AUGER

BEADED MITER

BEAUTIFUL MITER

SOLID TURRID

BARBADOS MITER

VARIABLE MITER

FLORIDA AUGER

COMMON AMERICAN AUGER

FLORIDA MITER

FLAME AUGER

In nature, most shells are abundant. Their obscure habitats, such as deep water or inaccessible crevices, may make some hard to find, and therefore rare in collections. Some specimans sell for thousands of dollars.

Rare Shells

All from the C. John Finlay collection.

JEWEL SLIT-SHELL. 2'' (5 cm)
Pleurotomaria gemma Bayer, 1965. Caribbean; deepwater. Natural slit is short.

ARCHER'S LYRIA 2.5'' (5 cm)
Lyria archeri (Angas, 1865). Caribbean; deepwater.

HOWELL'S FIG SHELL. 1.5'' **(4 cm).** *Ficus howelli* Clench & Farfante, 1940. Deepwater; Caribbean.

HELEN'S MITER 4'' **(10 cm).** *Mitra helenae* Radwin & Bibbey, 1972. Caribbean

DENNISON'S MORUM 2'' (5 cm). *Morum dennisoni* (Reeve, 1842) Caribbean; east Florida.

Shell-Less Seashells

NUDIBRANCHS are
sea-slugs with
no shells. Usually
⅓'' to 2'' long.
*Hypselodoris
edenticulata*
(White, 1952).
Common. 2''

L. S. Eyster, photo

RAGGED SEA-HARE
4'' (10 cm) is common
in shallow bays
along west coast
of Florida. Feed
on algae.
*Bursatella
pleii* Rang, 1828.

Alice Barlow, photo

Jelly egg strands
of a sea-slug
(Elysia) laid
on seaweed frond.
Early shell in egg
is shed after
two weeks.

Paul Mikkelsen, photo

Tusk Shells

The small, tubular shells are open at both ends.
The tusks live buried in sand just offshore.
Some are smooth, others ribbed.
IVORY TUSK, 2'' (5 cm). Carolinas to Texas.
Dentalium eboreum Conrad, 1846. Common.

Chitons

Distantly related to the snails, the rock-dwelling chitons (Polyplacophora) have 8 shelly plates bound at the edges by a leathery girdle.

FLORIDA SLENDER CHITON. 1''
(2.5 cm). *Stenoplax floridana*
(Pilsbry, 1892). Florida Keys.
Common under reef rocks.

HEMPHILL'S CHITON. 1''
(2.5 cm). *Craspedochiton hemphilli* (Pilsbry, 1893).
Subtidal under dead coral.

ROUGH-GIRDLED CHITON. 2''
(5 cm). *Ceratozona squalida* (C.B. Adams, 1845). Shore rocks; common. Caribbean.

COMMON EASTERN CHITON. ½''
Chaetopleura apiculata (Say, 1830). Eastern U.S. Subtidal, on shells and rocks; common.

FUZZY CHITON. 2½'' (6 cm). *Acanthopleura granulata*
(Gmelin, 1791). South Florida; West Indies. Shore rocky; common.

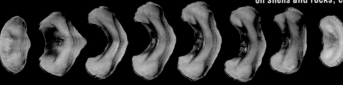

Underside of shelly valves removed from FUZZY CHITON.

Florida Tree Snails

These gorgeous, air-breathing snails are native to Florida, Cuba and Haiti. They feed on lichens growing on the bark of trees. One species, with many color varieties, occurs in the Everglades National Park where they are protected. *Liguus fasciatus* (Müller, 1777). 2'' (5 cm).

OPPOSITE PAGE: Over 50 color varieties of Florida Tree Snails, Liguus, are recognized. Some have recently become extinct after their habitat was destroyed. All natural size.

FLORIDA TREE SNAIL has four tentacles.

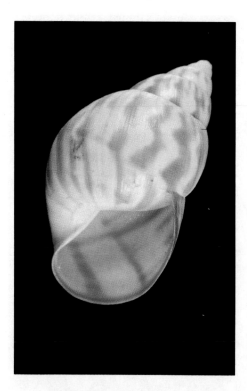

COY TREE SNAIL, *Orthalicus reses* Say, 1830 once from Key West is now extinct.

WAXY POLYGYRA is common Florida ground snail found in grass. 1/3'' (1 cm). *Polygyra cereolus* Mühlfeld. 1818

Florida
Fossils

Throughout central Florida there are many ''digs'' where fossil shells abound by the millions. Permission must be obtained to go on to private property.

Most of the fossils resemble today's kinds. Florida was under the sea during the Pliocene period about 20 million years ago.

Fossils are easy to collect and clean. This is the SCALY ARK, *Anadara scalarina* (Heilprin, 1887). 2'' (5 cm).

FLORIDA PLIOCENE FOSSILS

All natural size

1. WAGNER'S ARK, *Arca wagneriana* Dall, 1898.
2. HORRID VASE, *Vasum horridum* Heilprin, 1887.
3. SCALY TULIP, *Triplofusus scalarina* Heilprin, 1887.
4. SPINY JEWEL BOX, *Echinochama arcinella* L., 1767.
5. LION'S PAW, *Lyropecten nodosus* L., 1758.
6. ADVERSE CONE, *Conus adversarius* Conrad, 1849.
7. PROBLEM COWRIE, *Siphocypraea problematica* Heilprin, 1887.

COOPER'S ANODON 3'' (8 cm).
Anodonta coupêriana (Lea, 1840).
Common in ponds.

BUCKLEY'S PEARLY MUSSEL. 2½''
(6 cm). *Elliptio buckleyi* (Lea,
1843). Common in Florida lakes.

DURY'S RAMSHORN. ¾'' (2 cm).
Helisoma duryi (Wetherby, 1879).
Common in Everglade swamps.

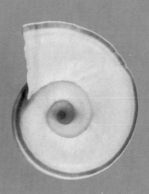

ROSY EUGLANDINA 1 - 2'' (4 cm).
Euglandina rosea (Ferussac, 1821)
Carnivorous ground snail.

RAMSHORN MARISA. 2'' (5 cm).
Marisa cornuarietis (L., 1758).
South Florida canals. Introduced from
South America in the 1950's. Has operculum.

KNOTTY CAMPELOMA. 1''
(2.5 cm). *Campeloma geniculum*
(Conrad, 1834). North Florida
streams; springs. Common.

GEORGIA APPLE SNAIL. 1''
Viviparus georgianus (Lea,
1834). Florida lakes
and streams. Common.

SWAMP APPLE SNAIL. 2'' (5 cm).
Pomacea paludosa (Say, 1829).
Everglade swamps. Food of birds.
Has horny operculum.

Pond, Lake and Land Shells

Courtesy of Harry G. Lee, M.C.

Nut Clams

The small nut clams have numerous, small teeth in the hinge. They are abundant in sandy, shallow areas, and are used in shellcraft. POINTED NUT CLAM, ⅓'' (10 mm). *Nuculana acuta* (Conrad, 1831).

Ark Clams

CUT-RIBBED ARK. 3'' (8 cm). *Anadara floridana* (Conrad, 1869). Carolinas to Texas. Offshore; common.

PONDEROUS ARK. 2'' (5 cm). *Noetia ponderosa* (Say, 1822). Virginia to Texas. Shallows; common.

BLOOD ARK. 2'' (5 cm). *Anadara ovalis* (Bruguière, 1789). Eastern U.S. Shallows; common.

TRANSVERSE ARK. 1'' *Anadara transversa* (Say, 1822). Eastern U.S. to Texas. Common.

MOSSY ARK. 1½'' (4 cm). *Arca imbricata* (Brug., 1789). S.E. U.S.; to Brazil. Common.

RED-BROWN ARK. 1'' (2.5 cm). *Barbatia cancellaria* (Lam., 1819). S.E. Florida.

ZEBRA ARK. 2 - 3''. (6 cm). *Arca zebra* (Swainson, 1833). S.E. U.S. to Brazil. Common.

Scallops have dozens of eyes along the mantle edge. When frightened, the scallop snaps its valves and swims away. BAY SCALLOP, 2½'' (6 cm), *Argopecten gibbus* (Linnaeus, 1758). Only the internal, round muscle is eaten.

ZIGZAG SCALLOP, 3'' (8 cm). *Pecten ziczac* (Linnaeus, 1758). Carolinas to Florida to Brazil. Shallow water, over sand. Common.

Lion's Paw Scallop

Color variations of the LION'S PAW, 2 - 4'' (10 cm).
Lyropecten nodosus (Linnaeus, 1758). Carolinas
to Texas; West Indies. Offshore; common.

LITTLE KNOBBY SCALLOP. 1½'' (4 cm).
Chlamys imbricatus (Gmelin, 1791)
S.E. Florida; West Indies. Among
subtidal coral rocks. Uncommon.

WAVY-LINED SCALLOP. 2'' (5 cm).
Aequipecten lineolaris (Lamarck,
1819). Off S.E. Florida and
Caribbean. Uncommon.

TRYON'S SCALLOP. 2'' (5 cm).
Aequipecten glyptus (Verrill,
1882). Eastern U.S. to Texas.
Deepwater; uncommon.

PAPER SCALLOP. 2'' (5 cm).
Amusium papyraceum (Gabb,
1873). Gulf of Mexico; deepwater.
Common.

ZIGZAG SCALLOP. 3'' (8 cm).
Pecten ziczac (Linnaeus,
1758). Carolinas to Brazil.
Offshore; common.

RAVENEL'S SCALLOP. 2'' (5 cm)
Pecten raveneli Dall, 1898.
Carolinas to Texas; West
Indies. Offshore; common.

Color variations of the CALICO SCALLOP, *Argopecten gibbus* (Linnaeus, 1758). 2''
Commercially trawled on both sides of Florida. The shells are popular in shell craft.

ROUGH SCALLOP. 1½'' (4 cm). *Aequipecten muscosus* (Wood, 1828). Carolinas to Brazil. Yellow form is rare.

TEREINUS SCALLOP 1''
Pecten chazaliei
Dautz., 1900. Rare.

PAPER SCALLOP 1''
(young). *Amusium papyraceum* (Gabb, 1873). Deepwater.

SENTIS SCALLOP. 1½'' (4 cm). *Chlamys sentis* (Reeve, 1853). Carolinas to Brazil. Subtidal, sides of rocks. Common.

ORNATE SCALLOP. 1½'' (4 cm).
Chlamys ornata (Lamarck, 1819).
S.E. Florida to Brazil.
Reef waters, under ledges. Uncommon.

Thorny Oysters

ATLANTIC THORNY OYSTER. 2 - 5'' (12 cm). *Spondylus americanus* (Hermann, 1781). S.E. U.S. Common. Offshore, attached to cliffs and wrecks. Beauties are rare.

Nearly all bivalves are
edible. (exception: Jingle Shells).
These few have been
commercially exploited in Florida.

Edible Bivalves

young, called ''cherrystone''

HARDSHELL CLAM or QUAHOG. 3''
Mercenaria mercenaria (Linnaeus,
1758). Shallow bays, lagoons. Common.

CALICO SCALLOP 2½'' (6 cm).
Argopecten gibbus (Linnaeus, 1758)

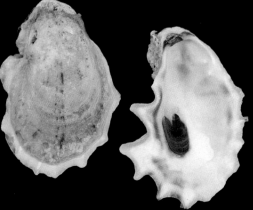

EDIBLE OYSTER 2 - 4'' (8 cm)
Crassostrea virginica (Gmelin, 1791).
Common in low saline bays.

SUNRAY VENUS. 6'' (15 cm).
Macrocallista nimbosa
(Lightfoot, 1786). Common
in N.W. Florida, offshore.

Beach habitat of the COQUINA CLAM.

Multicolored COQUINA Clams.

Coquina Clams

The COQUINA, Wedge, or Bean Clams live in great numbers on the slopes of sandy beaches in most parts of Florida. *Donax variabilis* Say, 1822. ½ - ¾'' (1.2 cm). Eastern U.S.

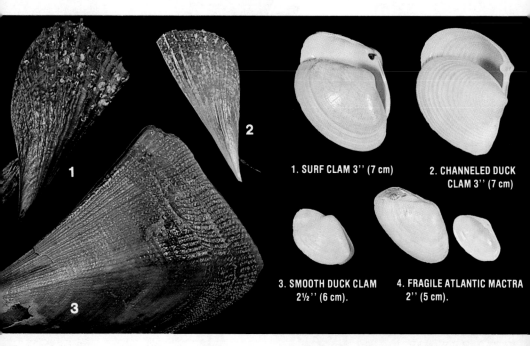

1. SURF CLAM 3'' (7 cm)

2. CHANNELED DUCK CLAM 3'' (7 cm)

3. SMOOTH DUCK CLAM 2½'' (6 cm).

4. FRAGILE ATLANTIC MACTRA 2'' (5 cm).

Pen Shells

1. STIFF PEN SHELL. 10'' (26 cm).
   Atrina rigida (Lightfoot. 1786)

2. AMBER PEN SHELL. 6'' (15 cm).
   Pinna carnea Gmelin. 1791.

3. SAW-TOOTHED PEN. 10'' (26 cm).
   Atrina serrata (Sowerby, 1825).

Mactra Clams

1. *Spisula solidissima* subspecies *similis* (Say, 1822). S.E. U.S.

2. *Raeta plicatella* (Lamarck, 1818). Carolinas to Texas to Argentina.

3. *Anatina anatina* (Spengler, 1802). Carolinas to Brazil.

4. *Mactra fragilis* Gmelin, 1791. Carolinas to Texas and West Indies.

Pearl Oysters & Mussels

1. *Pinctada imbricata* Röding, 1798.
   South Florida to Brazil. Common. 3''

2. *Pteria colymbus* (Röding, 1798).
   Carolinas to West Indies. Common. 2''

3. *Geukensia demissa* (Dillwyn, 1817).
   Eastern U.S. common in marshes. 2''

4. *Modiolus americanus* (Leach, 1815).
   Carolinas to Brazil. Offshore. 2''

5. *Lima lima* (Linnaeus, 1758).
   S.E. Florida to Brazil. Subtidal. 1''

6. *Brachidontes modiolus*
   (Linnaeus, 1767).
   South Florida. ½''

7. *Lima scabra* (Born, 1778).
   Carolinas to Brazil. 2''

1. ATLANTIC PEARL OYSTER. 3'' (7 cm).

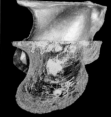

2. ATLANTIC WING OYSTER   3. RIBBED MUSSEL   4. TULIP MUSSEL

5. SPINY LIMA   6. YELLOW MUSSEL   7. ROUGH LIMA

. LEFT-HANDED JEWEL BOX 1½''

2. LEAFY JEWEL BOX 1½''

3. INEZ'S JEWEL BOX 1''

4. SPINY JEWEL BOX 1½''

5. CRESTED OYSTER. 2''. Two shapes.

Jewel Boxes & Crested Oysters

1. *Pseudochama radians* (Lamarck, 1819).
   Carolinas to Texas; West Indies.

2. *Chama macerophylla* (Gmelin, 1791).
   Carolinas to Brazil. Common.

3. *Pseudochama inezae* Bayer, 1943.
   Southeast Florida. Offshore; rare.

4. *Arcinella arcinella* (Linnaeus, 1767). S.E. U.S. to Brazil.

5. *Lopha frons* (Linnaeus, 1758).
   Florida to Brazil. Offshore.

Lucina Clams

The five species here are all found in shallow Florida waters and are all common.

AMERICAN TIGER LUCINA
3'' (7 cm). *Codakia orbicularis* (L., 1758).

BUTTERCUP LUCINA
2'' (5 cm). *Anodontia alba* Link, 1807.

THICK LUCINA. 2''
Lucina pectinata (Gmelin, 1791).

PENNSYLVANIA LUCINA
2'' (5 cm). *Linga pensylvanica* (l., 1758).

CROSS-HATCHED LUCINA
½'' (1.2 cm). *Divaricella quadrisulcata* (Orb., 1842).

Semele Clams

All three Florida species are common.

PURPLISH SEMELE. 1''
Semele purpurascens (Gmelin, 1791).

WHITE ATLANTIC SEMELE
1½''. *Semele proficua* (Pulteney, 1799).

CANCELLATE SEMELE
½''. *Semele bella-striata* (Conrad, 1837).

Jingles

JINGLE SHELLS are commonly attached to submerged wood and stones. Bottom valve has large hole. Flesh very bitter to taste.

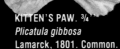

COMMON JINGLE SHELL
1''. *Anomia simplex* Orbigny, 1842. Common.

KITTEN'S PAW. ¾''
Plicatula gibbosa Lamarck, 1801. Common.

Cockles

VAN HYNING'S COCKLE from west Florida. 3 - 5''.

EVEN COCKLE 2½'' (6 cm). *Trachycardium isocardia* (Linnaeus, 1758). S.E. Florida to West Indies. Shallow water; common.

PRICKLY COCKLE. 2'' (5 cm). *T. egmontianum* (Shutt., 1856). Carolinas to Florida.

GIANT ATLANTIC COCKLE. 5'' *Dinocardium robustum* Lightfoot, 1786). N.E. FL.

STRAWBERRY COCKLE 1'' *Americardia media* (Linnaeus, 1758).

VAN HYNING'S COCKLE. 5'' *D. vanhyningi* Clench & Smith 1944. West coast of Florida.

EGG COCKLE. 2'' (5 cm). *Laevicardium laevigatum* (Linnaeus, 1758). Carolinas to Brazil. Common.

SPINY PAPER COCKLE 1'' (2.3 cm). *Papyridea soleniformis* (Brug., 1789) Carolinas to Brazil.

YELLOW COCKLE. 2'' (5 cm). *Trachycardium muricatum* (Linnaeus, 1758). Shallow water; common.

53

Venus Clams

1. ELEGANT DOSINIA 2½''

2. DISK DOSINIA. 3''

3. IMPERIAL VENUS. 1''

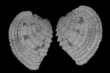

4. CALICO CLAM. 3''

5. SUNRAY VENUS. 5''

6. LADY - IN - WAITING VENUS 2''

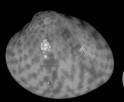

7. CROSS-BARRED VENUS. 1''

8. LIGHTNING VENUS. 1½''

9. PRINCESS VENUS. 3''

1. *Dosinia elegans* Conrad, 1846.

2. *Dosinia discus* (Reeve, 1850).

3. *Chione latilirata* (Conrad, 1841).

4. *Macrocallista maculata* (L., 1758).

5. *Macrocallista nimbosa* (Lightfoot).

6. *Chione intapurpurea* (Conrad, 1849).

7. *Chione cancellata* (Linnaeus, 1767).

8. *Pitar fulminata* (Menke, 1828).

9. *Periglypta listeri* (Gray, 1838).

Most of these species of Venus clams are common in sand in shallow waters.

Other Bivalves

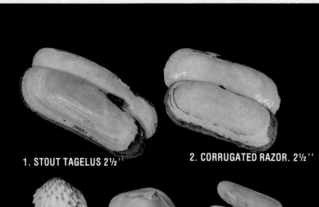

1. STOUT TAGELUS 2½''

2. CORRUGATED RAZOR. 2½''

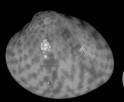

5. PURPLISH TAGELUS. 1''

3. BROAD-RIBBED CARDITA. 1''   4. GIBB'S CLAM. 2''

7. POINTED VENUS. ½''

6. GIANT FALSE DONAX. 2''

8. GAUDY ASAPHIS. 2''

1. *Tagelus plebeius* (Lightfoot, 1786). Eastern U.S. to Brazil. Mud flats.

2. *Solecurtus cumingianus* Dunker, 1861. Carolinas to Brazil; offshore.

3. *Carditamera floridana* Conrad, 1838. Florida to Mexico. Shallow sands.

4. *Eucrassatella speciosa* (A. Adams, 185 Carolinas to West Indies. Offshore.

5. *Tagelus divisus* (Spengler, 1794). Eastern U.S. to Brazil. Shallow water

6. *Iphigenia brasiliana* (Lam., 1818). South Florida to Brazil. Shallows.

7. *Anomalocardia auberiana* (Orbigny, 1842). Florida - Texas.

8. *Asaphis deflorata* (Linnaeus, 1758). S. Florida to Brazil. Intertidal sand.

SPECKLED TELLIN. 3'' (7 cm). *Tellina listeri* Röding, 1798. Carolinas to Brazil. Offshore; common.

ROSE PETAL TELLIN 1½'' (4 cm). *Tellina lineata* Turton, 1819. Florida to Texas.

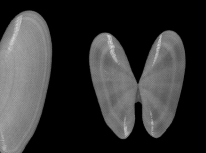

SUNRISE TELLIN. 2'' (5 cm). *Tellina radiata* Linnaeus, 1758. Carolinas to West Indies. Offshore coral sands. Common.

WHITE-CRESTED TELLIN. 1½'' (4 cm). *Tellidora cristata* (Recluz, 1842). Carolinas to Florida to Texas. Shallow sands; uncommon.

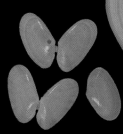

ALTERNATE TELLIN. 2½'' (6 cm). *Tellina alternata* Say, 1822. Carolinas to Texas. Shallow water; common.

CANDY STICK TELLIN. 1'' (2.5 cm). *Tellina similis* Sowerby, 1806. South Florida and Caribbean. Shallow waters; common.

ANGULATE TELLIN. 2'' (5 cm). *Tellina angulosa* Gmelin, 1791. South half of Florida to Brazil. Shallow water; common.

55

Angel Wings

ANGEL WINGS (3 - 5'') are common in mud in shallow bays of Florida. Top of hinge has a separate plate. Inside has a ''spoon''. *Cyrotopleura costata* (Linnaeus, 1758).

Angel Wings have a long siphon. The shell is covered with an outer gray ''skin''. One must dig down about two feet to collect them.

Paul Mikkelsen, photo

Argonauts & Spirula (Cephalopods)

BROWN PAPER NAUTILUS. 1½''.
Argonauta hians Lightfoot, 1786.
Shells are egg cases of pelagic octopus.

COMMON PAPER NAUTILUS. 6''
Argonauta argo Linnaeus, 1758. Pelagic

ACKNOWLEDGMENTS

he shells illustrated in this book were
indly loaned by C. John Finlay, Gloria
carboro, Minnie Lee Campbell, Harry G.
ee, Lois Salvay and Cecelia W. Abbott.
pecial thanks go to Roberta Cranmer and
nne and David Joffe.

SPIRULA shells come ▶
from dead, deepsea
squid. They float ashore.
Spirula spirula L. 1758. 1''.

Courtesy of Neil Hepler

Collecting Shells

Intertidal mud flats harbor many live shells. Collect at low tide and at night.

Snails leave trails. Bivalves have one or two holes to reveal their presence below.

Along rocky shores at low tide are found periwinkles and nerites in pools.

The 8-plated chitons are vegetarians that roam over rocks at night.

Some beaches, especially at Sanibel Island, have dead shells after a N.W. storm.

In the Gulf Stream, sargasso weed floats and supports crabs, fish and snails.

Snorkling for shells in shallow waters can bring rich rewards. Return overturned rocks.

Small or large dredges pulled from a boat over bottom at 10 to 80 feet bring rarities.

Look for shells everywhere — both sides
of horseshoe crabs, on dead shells, in wood
logs, under rocks and in sponges.

Do not over-collect any species. There
is a size and bag limit for Florida Pink,
or Queen, Conchs, and unlawful to collect
live corals or seafans. Consult local laws.

Cleaning Shells

To clean shells, start water cold,
boil for 10 minutes, then slowly cool.
Freezing overnight, then thawing, also works.

Twist out meat (sliced and pounded
foot of big snails is edible). Save
trapdoor. Clean shell with brush.

Storing Shells

Keep accurate locality data and habitat
information on neat labels to go with
cleaned shells. Plastic bags, open boxes,
glass-covered cases, or more advanced
cabinets with sliding, shallow drawers
can be used. Put small shells in bags
or glass vials with cotton plug. Get
"Standard Catalog of Shells" by Wagner
and Abbott, which has blank catalog sheets.

Life Cast Ashore

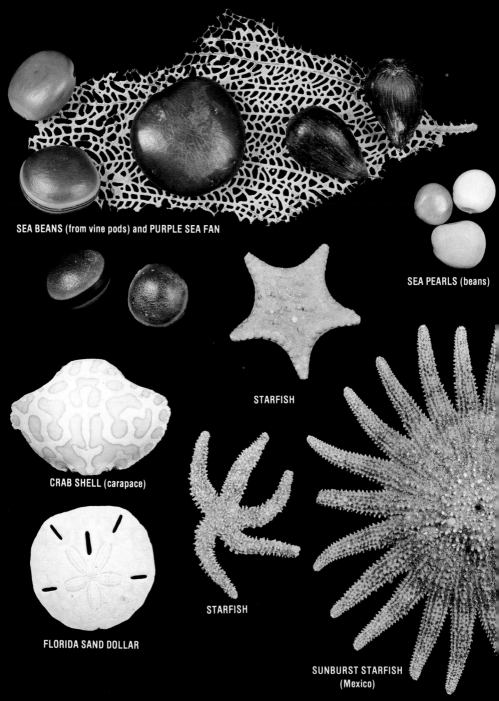

SEA BEANS (from vine pods) and PURPLE SEA FAN

SEA PEARLS (beans)

STARFISH

STARFISH

CRAB SHELL (carapace)

FLORIDA SAND DOLLAR

SUNBURST STARFISH
(Mexico)

Life Cast Ashore

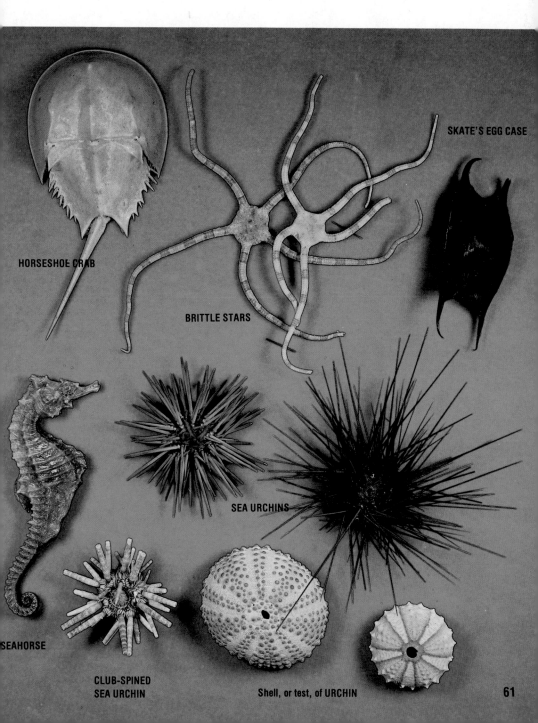

SKATE'S EGG CASE

HORSESHOE CRAB

BRITTLE STARS

SEA URCHINS

SEAHORSE

CLUB-SPINED
SEA URCHIN

Shell, or test, of URCHIN

61

COWRIE-HELMET. 2'' (5 cm)
Cypraecassis testiculus
(Linnaeus, 1758). S.E. FL
and West Indies. Uncommon.

COMMON FIG SHELL. 3'' (7 cm).
Ficus communis Röding, 1798.
Carolinas to Texas. Common
in shallow water; sand.

CHANNELED TURBAN. 3'' (7 cm).
Turbo canaliculatus Hermann,
1781. Lower Florida Keys to
Brazil. Uncommon; rocks.

Marine HERMIT CRABS use shells as temporary homes.

HERMIT CRAB IN
SCOTCH BONNET SHELL

More About Shells

THIS BOOKLET covers only a few hundred of the 3,000 kinds of shells that can be found in Caribbean shallow and deep waters. Your public library, school or local book dealer may have several of the many dozens of excellent books on conchology. You may also write for books available through reliable mail-order: American Malacologists, Inc., P.O. Box 2255, Melbourne, Florida 32902 U.S.A.

MANY PERMANENT EXHIBITS on shells are on display at the Bailey-Matthews Shell Museum on Sanibel Island, southwest Florida. Phone: (813) 395-2233.

CARIBBEAN SEASHELLS by Germaine L. Warmke and R. Tucker Abbott, 1975. 348 pp., 44 pls. (4 in color), maps. Inexpensive paperback, Dover Publ., N.Y.

SEASHELLS OF NORTH AMERICA by R. Tucker Abbott, Revised, 1986. Inexpensive paperback guide to identification of 850 species. Golden Press, N.Y.

KINGDOM OF THE SEASHELL by R. Tucker Abbott, 1982. Best introduction to the hobby and biology of mollusks. 256 pp. Many color plates. Bonanza Books, N.Y.

COMPENDIUM OF SEASHELLS by R. Tucker Abbott and S. Peter Dance, 1986. Largest color guide to 4,200 worldwide marine species. Large bibliography on shells. American Malacologists, Inc., Melbourne, FL

COMPENDIUM OF LANDSHELL by R. Tucker Abbott, 1989. 240 pp., 2,100 species in color of worldwide woodland and tree snails. American Malacologists, Inc.

PLIOCENE MOLLUSCA OF SOUTHERN FLORIDA by A. Olsson and Ann Harbison, 1953. (1990 reprint). 457 pp., 65 pls. Bailey-Matthews Shell Museum, Sanibel, FL 33957.

SHELLS OF THE ATLANTIC & GULF COASTS & THE WEST INDIES by R. Tucker Abbott & Percy Morris. 4th edition, 1995. Houghton Mifflin, Boston.

Allan B. Walker, photo

Thirty nationwide, annual shell shows, many of which take place in Florida, are educational and further the interests of conchology.

Index